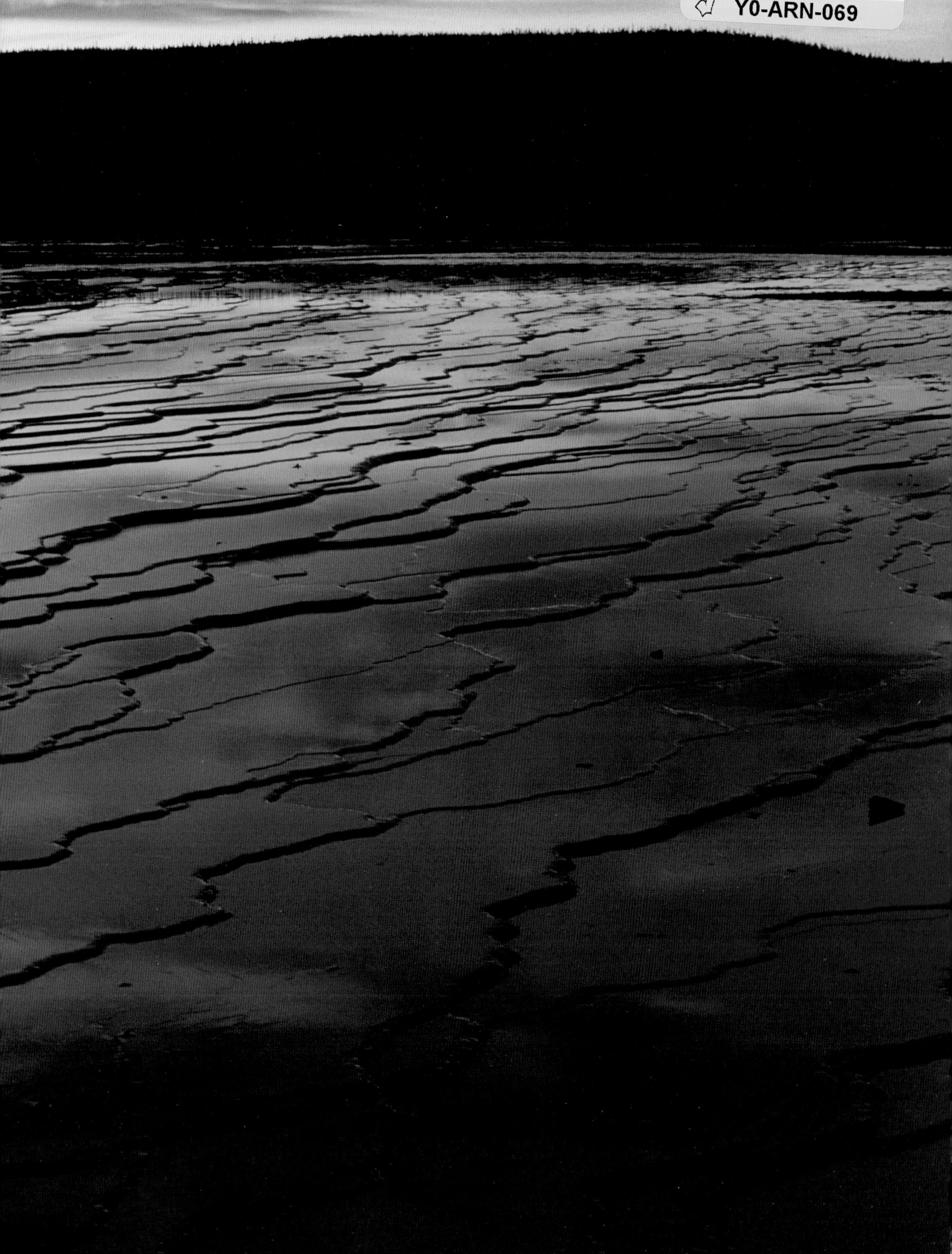

A LIVING LEGACY

yellowstone

NATIONAL PARK

Produced for Hamilton Stores, Inc., and TW Recreational Services, Inc.
by Sequoia Communications, Santa Barbara, CA.

Contributing Editor: Carey Vendrame
Contributing Writer: David Swift
Design by Adine Maron
Map by Karen Hubbard
Production assistance by Marcus Graczyk
Type by Graphic Traffic, Santa Barbara, CA
Printed in Hong Kong

ISBN: 0-917859-99-5
First printing, 1989

Special thanks to Tim Manns, North District Naturalist and Park Historian, Division of Interpretation, Yellowstone National Park, for his review of the manuscript.

PHOTOGRAPHY

Frank Balthis: P. 2, 5, 22 top left, inside back cover—right. *Ed Cooper:* P. 30 bottom, 32 bottom, 41, 43 top, inside back cover—top left. *Dennis Cwidak:* P. 19 top, 36 bottom. *Michael Francis:* P. 3, 6-7, 14 top left, 18 top & bottom, 20 left, 22 middle & bottom left, 26 bottom left, 37, 46 bottom, inside back flap (paperback edition). *Jeff Gnass:* Front cover, P. 31 top & bottom right, 38 top. *Haynes Foundation Collection, Montana Historical Society, Helena Mont.:* P. 10, 11 top & bottom, 12 top & bottom, 13, 42-43. *Jeff Henry:* Inside back cover—bottom left. *Philip Hyde:* P. 24-25. *Frank Jensen:* P. 18 middle, 38 bottom, 44 top. *Lewis Kemper:* P. 22 bottom right, 34 top, 42, 46 top. *Sandy Nykerk:* Front flap, P. 6, 8, 16 top, 24 top, 26 top left & bottom right, 29 bottom, 30 top. *Wayne Scherr:* P. 32 middle, 44-45. *Diana Stratton:* P. 14 top right. *John Telford:* P. 27, 43 bottom, 47. *Glenn Van Nimwegen:* Inside front cover-P. 1, 2-3, 8-9, 14-15, 16 middle & bottom, 17, 19 bottom, 20 right, 21, 23, 28, 29 top, 30 middle, 31 bottom left, 33, 34-35, 36 top, 39, 40 top & bottom. *Kennan Ward:* Back cover. *Ted Wood:* P. 32 top.

INSIDE COVER: *Sunset at Grand Prismatic Spring.* **RIGHT:** *West Thumb Geyser Basin.*

TABLE OF

contents

CREATED BY
ACT OF CONGRESS
MARCH 1, 1872

A visit to Yellowstone National Park confirms in anyone's mind that uninhabited wilderness is indeed a national treasure. The park's 2,219,785 acres of spacious valleys and vast backcountry are a stronghold for wildlife, and its world-famous features are reminiscent of primeval times.

Over 80 million people have experienced Yellowstone's wonders since it became a national park in 1872, but the Yellowstone Plateau has been home to man for a very long time. Stone articles and ancient campsites found in some areas of Yellowstone suggest that humans have inhabited the area for most of the 8,500 years since the last ice age. The area was traversed by a number of Indian groups, including the Crow, Blackfeet, Shoshone, and Bannock. A group known as the Sheepeaters was the only one to actually take up year-round residence in the area that is now Yellowstone National Park. As their name suggests, they hunted the mountain sheep in the park's rugged areas and had no horses or firearms.

An Indian tribe, the Minnetaree Sioux, is thought to be responsible for the origin of Yellowstone's name. After viewing the cliffs along the lower Yellowstone River, they called the area "Mi-tsi-a-da-zi" or Rock Yellow Water. Later, French trappers called it "Pierre Jaune" or "Roches Jaunes," meaning Yellow Stone or Yellow Rocks, respectively.

John Colter, a member of the Lewis and Clark expedition, is believed to have been the first white person to view and report on the wonders of Yellowstone. In 1807, Colter took leave from the expedition to do some independent exploring. His travels took him, historians presume, from the mouth of the Big Horn River up the Yellowstone River, over to the Shoshone River, over Union Pass between the Wind River and Gros Ventre Range, to Jackson Hole, over Teton Pass, and then north to Yellowstone.

So what was to become of this extraordinary area? Trapping took place from approximately 1813 to the 1830s. Prospectors passed through in the 1860s, but mining began *outside* the park. People first began claiming hot springs in 1871 in hopes of cashing in on their restorative properties. Scientific exploration began with the Hayden Survey in 1871. All were fully aware, as pioneer Nathaniel P. Langford observed, that Yellowstone "would eventually become a source of great profit to the owners."

Intrigued by "marvelous tales of burning plains, immense lakes, and boiling springs," a group of explorers, under the auspices of Henry D. Washburn, surveyor general of Montana, set out in 1870 on an expedition to the area.

CHAPTER • 1

yellowstone's beginnings

PREVIOUS PAGE, TOP: *Detail from the Theodore Roosevelt Arch, at the North Entrance.* **BOTTOM:** *The breathtaking Grand Canyon of the Yellowstone.*

ABOVE: *Visitors to Yellowstone have been awed by Old Faithful for many years.* **OPPOSITE, TOP:** *A party of climbers at Mammoth, circa 1895.* **BOTTOM:** *A day party with horse-drawn coach stops at Liberty Cap, Mammoth Hot Springs, year unknown.*

It has been suggested that members of the Washburn party sat around the campfire one evening discussing the future of this magnificent place they had explored. As the story goes, Cornelius Hedges, an attorney and member of the group, spoke up and discouraged exploitation and private ownership of the area and proposed that it be held by the government for the use and enjoyment of the people. The others agreed and together they outlined a campaign to make Yellowstone a national park.

The idea was not a completely new one, discussions of creating national parks date back to the 1830s. And in 1864, concerned, influential citizens and officials in California had banded together to lobby in Congress for preservation of the Mariposa Grove, the giant sequoia forest near Yosemite Valley, which was being devastated by lumber companies, and for protection of the valley itself. As a result of their efforts President Lincoln signed into effect the Yosemite Land Grant in 1864, making Yosemite America's first state park. The precedent was set. This precedent for setting aside federal land for preservation in its natural state was a significant one.

In the months following the Yellowstone expedition, Cornelius Hedges wrote an article for the Helena *Daily Herald,* while fellow explorer Nathaniel Langford traveled to the East Coast to deliver lectures to a curious public—all in an effort to gain support for the national park idea.

Inspired by Hedges' and Langford's endeavors, Dr. Ferdinand Vandiveer Hayden of the U.S. Geological Survey requested, and was granted, $40,000 to officially explore the area. In June 1871, Hayden and his party of 40 men, including respected geologists, biologists, and mapmakers, set out from Utah. Hayden invited painter Thomas Moran and photographer William H. Jackson along to capture the park's aesthetic qualities. Their photographs and paintings, along with Hayden's 500-page report, helped convince Congress to pass a bill that would make Yellowstone the country's first national park. The bill was signed into law by President Ulysses S. Grant on March 1, 1872.

The national park idea was not Hedges' alone. It was advocated by many, including Northern Pacific Railroad, which was expanding its routes. Later national parks, such as Yosemite in 1890 (protecting parts of the area not included in the Yosemite Land Grant), were also created as a consequence of business and conservation interests—a combination of the pragmatic and the romantic.

Nathaniel Langford received notice of his appointment as Yellowstone's first guardian on May 10, 1872. He was not paid and did not reside in the park. The Park Bill did not create guidelines for managing the park nor did it allocate money for its maintenance and protection. Consequently, between 1872 and 1886, Yellowstone fell victim to its visitors. Langford and subsequent superintendents were confronted with many problems, including vandalism, game poaching, and arson.

Finally, in 1886, the U.S. Army was given the responsibility of protecting and managing Yellowstone. The Army fulfilled this mission until the establishment of a new organization, the National Park Service, which was authorized by Congress on August 26, 1916. The U.S. Army remained in Yellowstone with the National Park Service until October 1918.

This organization established a new hierarchy to run the national parks. A superintendent had overall responsibility for each park and was to be assisted by a corps of rangers who were given the powers of civilian policemen. The Army superintendents were called "Acting Superintendents" and reported to both the Secretary of War and the Secretary of the Interior, who managed the parks.

ESTABLISHING A LEGACY

The National Park Service owed its existence to a persistent Chicago business tycoon, Stephen T. Mather, who was concerned about the fate of the national parks. He wrote to fellow college alumnus, Franklin K. Lane,

ABOVE: *Theodore Roosevelt Arch, circa 1903.*
RIGHT: *Orange Spring Mound in the Upper Terraces at Mammoth Hot Springs was named for the orange algae that streaks it, circa 1915.*

then-Secretary of the Interior, to complain about the way the parks were being run. Lane replied: "Dear Steve: If you don't like the way the national parks are being run, why don't you come down to Washington and run them yourself?"

Mather decided to do just that. In 1914, he and a young Interior Department lawyer, Horace Albright, started working together to improve conditions in the national parks. By 1916, they had gathered together enough supporters to steer a bill through Congress and the Senate, creating the National Park Service. Horace Albright went on to become the first National Park Service superintendent of the world's first national park—Yellowstone.

Yellowstone has always been a rugged place. In the early days, dusty, harrowing stagecoach rides were the order of the day for the "carriage trade" —the wealthier tourists who could afford such a thing. Those who toured in their own wagons were known as "sagebrushers." The Grand Loop, completed in 1905, was a six-day journey that featured screeching brakes and clattering horse hooves down desperate slopes. Initially, accommodations along the way consisted of a couple of tents and cabins with dirt floors, though by the turn of the century modest hotels began opening. A large hotel was built at Mammoth in 1883 and the Fountain Hotel was built in 1891.

SERVICES AND ACCOMMODATIONS

By the 20th century, magnificent hotels began to open in Yellowstone and park visitation boomed during Horace Albright's 10 years as superintendent (1919-1929). Mather and Albright had realized at an early stage that people would care less about preserving something they had never seen. Therefore, from the beginning, they encouraged tourism in order to fulfill the Park Service's mission to make the parks accessible to all the people. In Yellowstone, under Albright's tenure, automobiles became prevalent in the park, and visitation subsequently quadrupled, necessitating road improvements, service stations, campgrounds, and other services.

In order to protect Yellowstone's grandeur and abundant natural beauty, the National Park Service has had to carefully choose the concessioners that provide the park's various guest services. The four concessioners currently operating in Yellowstone are Hamilton Stores, Inc.; Yellowstone Park Division, TW Recreational Services, Inc.; Yellowstone Park Service Stations; and Yellowstone Medical Services. Hamilton Stores, a family-owned corporation, has been serving Yellowstone visitors since 1915, thereby qualifying it as one of the oldest concessions in the national park system. Hamilton Stores operates nine general stores, offering gifts, apparel, groceries, fishing/camping supplies and food service; five photo shops, including one-hour photo processing; and a tackle shop located at Bridge Bay Marina. TW Recreational Services, Inc. operates hotels, motor inns, restaurants, lodges, cabins, and provides transportation, bus tours, saddle horse trips, stagecoach rides, boat excursions and rentals, and fishing guide services.

BELOW: *Stagecoaches in front of the Mammoth Hotel at Mammoth Hot Springs, circa 1910.*

March in Yellowstone is not springtime—deep snows still cover the land. Much wildlife has migrated to the "banana belt," the more temperate portion of the park around Mammoth, Tower, and Lamar Valley, to find green grasses preserved under thinner snow cover.

Elk and deer look bedraggled, and move as if in slow motion as they systematically forage for the scant browse. Their fat reserves are being depleted so ribcages are distinct under their fur. Coyotes mingle freely in the midst of elk herds, taking note of the weak ones.

On the Firehole River, bison have their own method of grazing. They throw their large heads back and forth in a machine-like motion, as they plow through snow to uncover grasses, sedges, and forbs.

As the days become warmer, a black bear with cubs emerges from her den after a five-month hibernation. Though omnivorous, she scouts for carcasses of elk, bison, and deer, which will be the most plentiful protein available until the snow recedes.

As spring moves north—at the rate of 15 miles per day, they say—bears partake of insects, buds, shrubs, tubers, and rodents. Grizzlies, more so than black bears, snag fish from the river with a swipe of their long, curved claws. Insects and vegetation are important spring and summer foods for bear, and later in summer, huckleberries are stripped from the bush. Yellowstone's bounty provides well for its wildlife.

It is almost as if nature itself had intended Yellowstone National Park to become a game preserve. High grassy plains are sequestered in a secluded realm, supported by a never-ending source of water. Thousands of acres of dense lodgepole pine provide cover. Yellowstone was so far from civilization 100 years ago that by the time hunters discovered it, regulations were in place to protect its bounty. It was a close call; the gray timber wolf was eliminated and others remain threatened, but the worst is over.

The black bear is less aggressive but more abundant than the grizzly, which remains in danger of extinction. Black bears weigh up to 250 pounds or more, while a grizzly can weigh more than twice that. They share the same broad-based diet.

Both species vary greatly in color, from tan to black. The grizzly is distinguished from the black bear by its slightly concave face, much longer claws, a hump at the shoulders, and a blond to gray tinge on its longer hairs. Black bears and only young grizzlies climb trees. Researchers have learned that in their day-to-day roaming grizzlies may cover a radius of 50 miles. Most travel less than that on a day-to-day basis.

CHAPTER • 2

flora and fauna

PREVIOUS PAGE, TOP LEFT: *Black bear cub peeks over tree branch.* **TOP RIGHT:** *Great grey owl chick in nest.* **BOTTOM:** *Summertime wildflowers on Mt. Washburn.*

TOP: *A grazing bison provides a rest stop for some birds.* **MIDDLE:** *Battling bighorn rams.* **BOTTOM:** *Moose cow and calf exchange an affectionate touch.* **OPPOSITE:** *A bighorn sheep stands precariously on a ledge at Calcite Springs.*

Many are surprised to see the thousands of buffalo in Yellowstone, because they, too came perilously close to extinction. In 1902 there were about 40 left in the park. The park artificially cultivated the herd before turning it back to the completely natural existence it now enjoys.

Buffalo weigh as much as a ton and can accelerate like a falling rock. They appear docile and since Yellowstone's roads often pass through their habitat, injuries caused by charging buffalo sometimes occur. Once angered —and without warning—a buffalo will give its enemy a solid butt with its head, goring it with its horn. Since all animals in Yellowstone National Park are wild and potentially dangerous, visitors should keep a distance, out of respect for the animals and to insure their own safety.

Buffalo are the first large mammals to bear young in the spring. In May they give birth to calves that sport a red-orange coat, which turns dark brown by fall.

Elk are the most abundant species of large mammals, numbering over 30,000 in the summer. At dawn and at dusk they can be spotted at the edges of many meadows, as they forage on all types of vegetation, including grasses, shrubs, buds, and leaves.

Elk found in the northern part of the park spend the winter around Mammoth, Gardiner, northern areas outside the park, and Lamar Valley, an area known locally as "the banana belt" for its temperate climate. A second herd can be found wintering around the Firehole River and a third migrates south to Jackson Hole's National Elk Refuge. A fourth migrates to the Gallatin River and a fifth moves eastward, out of the park.

Elk calves are born in June and weigh 30 to 40 pounds. They are cloaked in a spotted camouflage fur. A mother protects her young by rearing and lashing out with her front hooves.

Bull elk grow to 700–1,000 pounds, and are characterized by a rack of antlers that undergoes a constant change. Each spring the rack falls off and is replaced by a nubbins. The growing antler is soft and tender, and the elk is said to be "in velvet."

By fall's mating season the rack is larger than it was a year before and the clattering sound of elk dueling—a ritual of dominance—can be heard in the meadows. Early mornings between first light and sunrise is the time to listen for the remarkable sound of bugling elk, a low, almost metallic bellow that increases in pitch.

Both the Dakota mule deer (or Blacktail deer), so called because of its ample ears, and the whitetail deer can be seen in the park, though the whitetail deer is scarce. Mature mulies weigh 100–400 pounds. They are not as abundant as elk nor do they congregate in herds, but often can be spotted in the same areas. Other than in winter, deer suffer their worst casualties at the hands of nighttime drivers. Unlike elk, deer often pause in the middle of the road, and sudden headlights can cause them to jump in the wrong direction.

In the summer, moose inhabit marshy areas such as along the Yellowstone River near Fishing Bridge, Hayden Valley, and the Lewis River near Lewis Falls, as well as very different places such as the slopes of Mt. Washburn. They nibble twigs and leaves and are often spotted wading in search of water lilies and submerged roots. A cow with young is a very protective animal and should be given a wide berth.

Mountain sheep inhabit the hills between Gardiner and Mammoth in winter, and move to higher elevations in the summer. They can also be found in the northwest corner near Soda Butte, and the Mt. Washburn area. Their sure-footedness is not a myth, in fact, modern-day rock climbers are in awe of the mountain sheep's ability to navigate precarious terrain. Both male and female sheep grow horns; the ram's tend to be robust with a curl, while the female's are more delicate. The sound of rams engaged in a butting contest sounds lethal but is usually harmless.

Pronghorn antelope are a common sight along sagebrush-covered flats in the northern parts of the park, and like sheep, both male and female

TOP: *The pronghorn antelope can make the white hair on its rump stand up to reflect light and flash warnings to other antelope.* **MIDDLE:** *A coyote stalks his prey.* **BOTTOM:** *Many Canada geese are year-round park residents.*

grow horns. They are capable of running 60 miles per hour in short bursts.

Mountain lions were hunted almost to extinction during Yellowstone's early years. Spotting one now is a most unusual occurrence as they are secretive hunters.

The coyote is a member of the dog family and is one of Yellowstone's primary carnivores. Over the years his stature among nature lovers has improved with an increased understanding of his role in the ecosystem. Rodents are his primary diet, but he also depends on weakening and dead ungulates in winter.

Like a cat, the coyote can stand motionless for minutes at a time stalking a meadow mouse. For those lucky enough to see the coyote in action, watching him pounce is worth the wait. He springs and then comes down on all fours.

Habituation of wildlife to people is a growing concern in Yellowstone. The Uinta squirrel, for instance, is so fearless that it scampers up to visitors and demands a handout. But since the park is a place where wildlife is to be preserved, feeding these animals is illegal and can be dangerous as well. Fish are the only living things that can legally be taken from the park. The Yellowstone cutthroat trout is native to the area, but four other species of trout have been introduced. In fact, when Yellowstone was established in 1872, 40% of its waters had no fish. As an attempt to improve the area, fish were introduced for sport, so there are now fish in Yellowstone where nature did not put them. Fishermen must have a license issued by the park (not the state) and should check regulations, as not all areas are open and some areas are strictly catch-and-release.

Yellowstone offers a great variety of habitats for the more than 200 different species of birds that reside in the park. Since birds and wildlife are protected here, they can live undisturbed and rear their young.

Many of the birds in Yellowstone are nature's most magnificent. Pelicans occur in fair numbers along the Yellowstone River and Fishing Bridge. The rare trumpeter swan breeds, among other places, at Indian Lake outside the southwest border of the park, and in the park. Only 10,000 exist in the world. Great blue herons are generally considered uncommon in Yellowstone, but they become common at some times of the year. Sandhill cranes have over 100 nests in Yellowstone and are also considered uncommon. The Canada goose is a very social bird that flocks to marshy areas around warm springs. The fortunate observer may sight the great grey owl at the margins of Yellowstone's meadows.

Slow or standing water in the Yellowstone and Firehole rivers, as well as many others, is a primary habitat for gulls, and numerous varieties of ducks (mergansers, teal, wigeon, mallards, and many more). Less common are grebes, loons, the snowy egret, and the double-crested cormorant.

Raptors are predatory birds that exist far and wide. The golden eagle nests on ledges of cliffs, while the bald eagle nests atop tall, dead pines next to waterways. They can be identified in flight flapping their wings in slow, powerful strokes as they circle at high elevations to scan the ground for rodents and hares and the rivers for ducks and fish. The bald eagle also eats carrion and fish. The osprey, a smaller bird, is similar in nesting habits, but feeds almost exclusively on fish. Of the park's many hawks, the red-tailed hawk is the most common.

The birds most likely to greet visitors are the Clark's nutcracker and the gray jay, commonly called, "camp robber." The gray jay is so adaptive that he'll approach snowmobilers in the dead of winter and eat out of their hands. This practice, however, is illegal and is not good for the birds. Gray with black on his head, the nutcracker's diet ranges from pine nuts to carrion. He joins the raven, magpie (with the long, black-and-white tail), and coyote as park scavengers.

Yellowstone is along the migratory path or is home to countless colorful birds—blithe spirits that twinkle in and out of sight in an instant. Any time in spring and summer might bring a

TOP: *A bald eagle is well camouflaged in this stand of trees along the Lamar River.*
BOTTOM: *A blue grouse displays its plumage.*

mountain bluebird, Western meadowlark, robin, mountain chickadee, junco, yellow warbler, killdeer, blue and ruffed grouse, or Western tanager flying through the park. The rosy finch is seen at low elevations (down to 6,000 feet) in the winter and only at the highest elevations (9,500 and up) during the summer.

WILDLIFE AND FOREST FIRES

The fires in the summer of 1988 gave people the opportunity to get a first-hand look at how animals react to fire. It is a myth that they run into the fire or over cliffs in blind panic. In fact, park wildlife was seen grazing and bedding down in smokey meadows, seemingly oblivious to the nearby blazes. Elk even licked ash from fallen trees for its nutrients. And after the fires, field rodents emerged from their insulated burrows, while birds began pecking new homes in the skeletons of blackened trees.

FLORA

Just as Yellowstone's diverse habitats provide for a variety of wildlife, there is also a wide variety of vegetation. The park's plant life includes aquatic communities, sagebrush deserts, alpine and subalpine meadows, four types of forests, and a plethora of wildflowers. Eighty percent of Yellowstone's land is forested. There are a few deciduous trees but most are conifers (cone-bearing).

The lodgepole pine is the most prominent form of plant life in Yellowstone. These trees are typically 60 or 70 feet tall and grow close together. As time goes by, a stand thins itself out, making it easy to ride a horse or walk between the lodgepoles. Pine bark beetles infest them, and can destroy acres at a time. The 1988 fires converted thousands of acres of lodgepole stands into areas for newer, more complex vegetation systems.

Other conifers include the limber pine, which is identified by five needles per bunch, and is found at altitudes around 6,000 feet. The Douglas fir has the largest trunk of any tree in the park (as much as six feet in diameter) and has pendant cones and flat, blunt needles. The Engelmann spruce is tall and symmetrical. Its needles are four sided and sharp and its bark is reddish colored.

Deciduous trees are few, with the aspen being the most plentiful. Squiggles in its leaves are an indication of an insect called "the leaf miner." Aspen leaves turn golden in the fall and their flat stems cause them to quiver in the breeze, hence the name "quaking aspen." Aspen bark is a favored food of elk and other animals.

Entire books have been devoted to Yellowstone's flowers. The Yellowstone Plateau becomes a carpet of vivid colors when wildflowers start to bloom in mid-June. Areas that appear sparsely covered from a distance explode with color as you approach them. Colors change constantly through July, when harder freezes begin to make life more difficult for fragile life forms.

Bitterroot is among the park's spring arrivals; its pink blossoms favor conditions on sagebrush flats. Phlox has tiny blue, white or pink petals, grows in moist, sunny spots, and is another spring arrival. It is one of the few Yellowstone flowers that you can smell before seeing it.

Lupine, larkspur, columbine, elephant head, Indian paintbrush (whose shade can vary from pink to crimson red) and fringed gentian (the official park flower) are among the park's most plentiful wildflowers. The magenta-colored fireweed is most conspicuous throughout the park when it blooms in late July.

Certain flowers demand special environments. The bright yellow and red monkeyflower grows next to streams. The evening primrose, whose blossoms open at sunset and close at sunrise, grows out of rock overhangs where it scarcely seems possible. The deep blue forget-me-not can only be seen by those heading for a mountain summit.

Somewhere between the plant and animal kingdoms, are algae, which are microscopic creatures whose formations and colors remind one of an abstract painting. Algae create many of the brilliant colors found at the edge of hot-spring runoffs. Porcelain Basin at Norris is heavily colored by green algae and minerals that can live in extremely hot water, a fact that interests biologists.

TOP: *Mountain bluebird.* **BOTTOM:** *The Rocky Mountain fringed gentian is Yellowstone's official flower.* **OPPOSITE:** *Monkey flowers on Mt. Washburn.*

TOP: *A cross-country skier stops to watch Old Faithful erupt on a cold (minus 35 degrees Fahrenheit) winter morning.* **MIDDLE:** *A bison cow and her calf romp in the snow.* **BOTTOM:** *An early fall snow storm.* **RIGHT:** *Snow-coach tours are a popular way to see the park in the winter.* **OPPOSITE:** *Lamar River.*

winter in yellowstone

Extreme heat and extreme cold, working in the overwhelming scale of geologic time, bear much responsibility for the creation of Yellowstone's wonders. What an utter delight it is to observe the improvisational performances of these elements during a Yellowstone winter.

Two-hundred-degree water erupts from a geyser, filling frigid air with steam. Azure skies are laced with brilliant white clouds. Rime—moist air quickly frozen—coats nearby trees, turning them into fairyland props. Hot springs declare their permanence in vivid relief against deep snowdrifts.

A Yellowstone winter arrives in late October or early November. By December snow covers the Plateau—12 inches often falls overnight, quietly, without fanfare. A snowpack of eight feet is not unusual, nor are 15-foot snowdrifts.

Once winter sets in it is unlikely that the temperature will rise above freezing for three months. From December through February lows are typically 10 degrees below zero and regularly hit 30 degrees below in the colder parts of the park. West Yellowstone, the western gateway town, routinely turns up in daily weather reports as the nation's coldest spot.

During the most bitterly cold months, animals are drawn to geyser basins along the Firehole River to be warmed by Yellowstone's thermal springs. Green shoots, though sparse, tide animals over the last few weeks of winter.

Of the nearly 2.5 million visitors annually, over 100,000 see Yellowstone in winter. Half of these tourists take to snow-covered park roads on snowmobiles. Others enter via over-snow vehicles at Mammoth, West Yellowstone, or Flagg Ranch. Mammoth Hot Springs Hotel and Snow Lodge at Old Faithful remain open year-round. All other overnight accommodations are closed between October and April. Shuttles (the world's only regularly scheduled over-snow bus service) from Mammoth Hot Springs Hotel take visitors to Norris Geyser Basin, Canyon, and other scenic attractions. The highway is plowed through Tower and Lamar Valley to Cooke City, Montana—a beautiful if sometimes icy drive.

Snow Lodge is a well-stocked resort with a restaurant that supplies remarkably fresh salads and entrees at competitive prices—even though the nearest competition is 30 snow-filled miles away. From Snow Lodge, daily shuttles take skiers and sightseers to such Yellowstone attractions as Mystic Falls (The shuttle doesn't go right to Mystic Falls so visitors must ski part way.) and the Grand Prismatic Spring.

Snowmobiling is limited to the park's paved roads. Gasoline is available at Canyon, Old Faithful, and Mammoth at the end of the plowed road. The park maintains warming huts at West Thumb, Canyon, Fishing Bridge, and Madison and Indian Creek. The huts provide brochures, a toasty wood stove, and vended coffee (not available at Fishing Bridge and Indian Creek).

Heightened interest in cross-country skiing has resulted in the establishment of more than 100 miles of developed ski trails. Ski packages are available at Old Faithful and Mammoth. Bulletin boards are updated daily regarding the ski conditions, as well as the best trails for spotting wildlife. Skiers are encouraged to watch out for hidden warm spots near geyser basins that can cause skis to ice up solid.

Skiing in Yellowstone carries a responsibility. While elk, bison, moose, and deer have become accustomed to traffic on park roads, they have not become accustomed to cross-country skiers. Skiers must therefore exercise the utmost consideration and keep a safe distance from wildlife.

Geologists regard Yellowstone as a remarkable phenomenon. In few other places is our planet's skin as thin. Yellowstone is virtually a window to the earth's inner workings.

The Yellowstone landscape has been eons in the making. Its oldest rocks were created 2.7 billion years ago. The youngest are being formed right now. The oldest rocks are metamorphic, which means that they were the result of great heat and pressure acting on existing rocks, forming new ones. These rocks may have begun as sedimentary (a layered rock resulting from the consolidation of sediment) or igneous rocks (formed by the solidification of cooling molten material).

A great deal of erosion and probably some uplifting occurred by 570 million years ago. Yellowstone was then essentially a flat plain. Rocks from this period can be seen on the Buffalo Plateau in the north part of the park.

For about 500 million years (about 570–75 million years ago) what are now known as the Pacific and Arctic oceans repeatedly flooded these flat, barren areas.

Sand and mud slowly covered these original sea beds and then solidified into sandstone and shale. Rocks from this time may be found on Mt. Everts, the Gallatin Mountains, and around the Snake River. Shells from mollusks, fossilized over countless centuries, are responsible for the limestone layers that are 300 feet deep in places. These and other sedimentary layers are visible where rivers have carved canyons. Fossils in the sandstone, shale, and limestone document life's evolution—from multi-celled invertebrates to the reptiles that roamed through the swampy forests that grew along the edge of the warm seas.

The Laramide Orogeny (refers to the development of the Rocky Mountains) began about 75 million years ago and lasted about 20 million years. As this period of mountain building continued, major crustal movements took place in Yellowstone and the Rocky Mountains. These crustal movements probably lead to the park's later volcanic events. Anticlines (a structural upfold in stratified rock, forming an arch), synclines (a structural downfold in stratified rock, forming a trough), and various faults date from this period. Uplifting movements during the mountain-building period changed stream courses and increased erosion.

There have been two major episodes of volcanic activity in Yellowstone. About 55–40 million years ago several large volcanoes erupted in and near Yellowstone. Eruptions produced volcanic rocks that formed the Absaroka and Washburn ranges and now cover part of the Gallatin Mountains, as well as other parts of Yellowstone.

CHAPTER • 3

yellowstone's unpredictable landscape

PREVIOUS PAGE, TOP: *Rhyolite lava near Craig Pass.* **BOTTOM:** *The spectacular Gallatin Mountains border the northwest corner of the park.*

TOP: *The remarkably blue Abyss Pool, West Thumb.* **BOTTOM:** *Petrified tree stump, Specimen Ridge.* **RIGHT:** *Mt. Washburn.* **OPPOSITE:** *A lava flow cooled to form these basalt columns.*

Intrusive rocks (formed within the earth's crust) and extrusive rocks (formed from cooling lava at the earth's surface) date from this time, as do lava, ash, pumice, rhyolite (an acidic volcanic rock that is the lava form of granite), basalt (a fine-grained igneous rock that is dark grey to black in color), and breccia (rock consisting of coarse fragments of volcanic rock). Heavy rainfall at this time caused significant mudflows and landslides, which buried the trees now petrified on Specimen Ridge, in the Gallatin Mountains, and along many tributaries of the Lamar River.

Volcanoes in the Absaroka Mountain Range buried most of Yellowstone under thousands of feet of lava, breccia, and ash. Yellowstone turned into a plateau with a few volcanic peaks towering above it and slow-moving streams running through it, as a result of this extensive deposition. Yellowstone was probably not as high above sea level then as it is today and based on fossil records, its climate was warm and almost subtropical.

Ten million years ago another period of uplift occurred. (There are no examples within the park from the 25-million-year period between the Absaroka volcanoes and this time.) The Tetons and the Gallatins were uplifted thousands of feet, increasing drainage and erosion throughout that area. Yellowstone became characterized by sharply defined canyons, mountains, and tablelands, as the uplift continued.

The first eruption of two magma-filled chambers under Yellowstone occurred about 2 million years ago. The huge caldera that resulted was largely obliterated by a later eruption, which occurred 600,000 years ago. Having lost so much magma, the two chambers collapsed, leaving a second caldera that was several thousand feet deep and many miles in diameter. This caldera was roughly bounded by the Washburn Range, Flat Mountain, the Red Mountains, and the Madison Junction Bluffs.

Between 200,000 and 125,000 years ago a third caldera eruption took place in what is now the West Thumb of Yellowstone Lake. This "caldera within a caldera" is four miles wide and six miles long. Yellowstone's lowlands became filled with dust and ash from these caldera eruptions. In fact, only peaks as high as Bunsen Peak stood above the ash.

Much of the molten lava that continued to flow from the two magma chambers filled in the caldera but some ran over the rim. Lava flows of rhyolite now comprise the columns found along the road near Tower Fall. Also formed at this time was Obsidian Cliff, which was derived from lava flow outside the caldera area. The last of the lava flows took place about 60,000 years ago.

There were three periods of glaciation—or ice ages—in Yellowstone. The "Pre-Bull Lake" glaciation lasted from 300,000 to 180,000 years ago and the "Bull Lake" glaciation lasted from 125,000 to 45,000 years ago. These glaciers existed in Yellowstone while lava was flowing in other parts of the park.

The "Pinedale" glaciation lasted from 25,000 to 8,000 years ago and is better known than the other two because it obscured many of the changes that the two previous glaciations had caused and gave the present landscape much of its characteristic appearance. Icefields from the Absaroka and Gallatin ranges and from mountains north of the park contributed to the Pinedale glaciers that covered Yellowstone.

Glacier ice built up as much as 3,000 feet thick (over the Lake Basin) within the park. The only areas that escaped being glaciated were the highest ridges and the west edge of the park The glaciers, which consisted of ice and rock, gouged and smoothed the topography. As they melted, the glaciers left behind moraines (piles of rock and sand) and erratics (large boulders), often carrying them 25-30 miles. Glacier meltwater created streams and lakes, causing erosion and redistribution of sediments. Though some snowfields exist year-round in Yellowstone, there are presently no glaciers in the park. A few can still be found in the Tetons.

Yellowstone is among the most seismically active places in the country. In fact, in 1959 the Hebgen Lake vicinity was the site of one of the century's major earthquakes, which measured 7.8 on the Richter scale.

Yellowstone's geologic status is changing constantly. Land is being turned into soil by plants and frost, canyons are being cut by the forces of wind and water, and underground rock is being dissolved and brought to the surface by the heat and acid of the thermal features. Mountains may even be growing or settling. Even the streams and forests are only temporary aspects of Yellowstone's ever-changing landscape.

YELLOWSTONE'S FUTURE

On a larger scale, what could happen next? Geologists claim that there is nothing in particular keeping the Yellowstone Caldera dormant. It may be merely a matter of the pressure from below overcoming the weight of the rock from above, an equilibrium that could shift at any time. Yellowstone collects a great deal of rain and snow, providing for both the Snake and Yellowstone Rivers, as well as two tributaries of the Missouri River: the Madison and the Gallatin rivers. And if the planet should cool, Yellowstone could witness the glaciers of another ice age. Needless to say, future visitors to the park won't see the same place that you are experiencing now—Yellowstone's geologic events are ongoing!

ABOVE: *Sun and mist create a rainbow at Tower Fall.*

TOP: *The Yellowstone River flows placidly through the Hayden Valley.* **BOTTOM:** *Located near the outlet of Yellowstone Lake, Fishing Bridge is a popular place to watch the native cutthroat trout.*

yellowstone river

A RIVER FOR EVERY SEASON

The Yellowstone River has been in existence for two million years. At its beginning it resembled several other rivers in the vicinity that were slowly eroding channels through the volcanic rock. When the eruption occurred that formed the Yellowstone Caldera, the valley through which the Yellowstone River flowed was choked with volcanic ash. This material hardened and filled in the valley, causing the path of the river to change and the amount of water in it to diminish. Eventually, however, the river was restored to its original length and size. It recut its old channel and reached its former level in the canyon. The steady course of the Yellowstone River was again interrupted 300,000 years ago by 100,000 years of glaciation. But the glaciers that passed through the region moved across the canyon and not down it, so the path of the river, and the shape of the canyon were not greatly affected. The river, and Grand Canyon through which it flows, looked as they do today approximately 100,000 years ago.

TOP: *The roaring and hissing of fumaroles can be heard at Porcelain Basin.* **MIDDLE:** *The bubbling mudpots at Artist Paint Pots in Gibbon Canyon.* **BOTTOM:** *Travertine deposits on the lower terraces at Mammoth Hot Springs.*

yellowstone's hydrothermal features

From well-known Old Faithful® to the many bubbling mudpots, visitors are awestruck by Yellowstone's thousands of magnificent thermal features. These thermal features can be divided into three groups:

- Those that have a lot of water (hot springs and geysers)
- Those that have a limited amount of water (mudpots)
- Those that have steam but no liquid (fumaroles)

Bacteria, algae, and minerals are responsible for Yellowstone's colorful thermal waters. Pools that are too hot to allow the growth of algae and bacteria are usually blue from the daylight reflecting from the geyserite on the sides and bottoms of the pools.

Booklets and brochures that provide detailed explanations of Yellowstone's natural features are available at various thermal areas. Consult *Hamilton's Guide* for the heights and eruption schedules of specific geysers.

Note: Hot springs and geyser basins are fragile and unstable, so be sure to stay on the boardwalks and do not throw coins or other items into thermal areas.

FUMAROLE

A *fumarole* is a hole or vent in the earth's crust from which hot gases escape. When water from rain or snow seeps down and comes into contact with very hot rock, it flashes into steam. The sudden increase in volume produces the pressure that drives the gases from the vent.

MUDPOTS

Mudpots (also called mud springs, paint pots, or mud volcanoes) are actually fumaroles that lead to a basin below the water table. The bubbling action is caused by steam rising through ground water (usually acid) that has dissolved local rocks into clays.

HOT SPRINGS

Technically, all hydrothermal features in Yellowstone are *hot springs,* but the term is commonly used to describe two specific types of hot springs: the springs that flow and form terraces, such as those at Mammoth, and the springs that appear as pools of hot water in many of the geyser basins. At Mammoth Hot Springs the underground "plumbing system" runs through relatively soft limestone. Great pressures do not build up as they do in geysers because of the soft rock and numerous openings to the surface. Instead, carbon dioxide gas coming from the hot volcanic rocks below the surface bubbles up through subterranean ground water, forming carbonic acid.

The hot acid quickly dissolves large quantities of limestone. The Mammoth Hot Springs are formed where lime-saturated water has seeped downward and out onto the surface. On the surface, the acid cools, giving off carbon dioxide gas, so the limestone is no longer in solution. It is precipitated to form the travertine (dissolved limestone that is deposited in small crystals) terraces.

The hot springs in the form of pools are found in geyser basins and are similar to geysers except that they do not erupt. These hot springs dissipate enough heat by boiling and by surface evaporation that they avoid the tremendous steam explosions that cause a geyser to erupt. Also, water cooled on the pool's larger surface settles down into the "plumbing system" and helps maintain an equilibrium. Even slight changes in this system or in the heat source can cause a hot pool to become a geyser, or vice versa.

GEYSERS

Geysers are hot springs that periodically spout heated water into the air. Such an eruption is caused by a steam explosion in the geyser's underground system that pushes water through narrow rock fractures with great force. Geysers are a rare phenomenon; in fact, only 10% of Yellowstone's hot springs are true geysers.

This is how they work: Ground water that has been heated by molten rock far below the surface is forced back up by cool water, which has seeped down through fractures in the bedrock.

As the water rises, it enters the geyser's "plumbing system," which consists of a maze of cracks and fissures in the subterranean rock that have become lined with geyserite. But the tremendous weight of the water in the column above it forces down and pressurizes the hot water as it tries to rise up through the "plumbing system." The water becomes heated to a temperature far above the boiling point (as in a pressure cooker). Since the pressure is so great, the water in the lower regions of the column cannot form the gas bubbles characteristic of boiling water—despite temperatures of 500-600 degrees Fahrenheit.

However, at a critical point, temperature and pressure are such that steam bubbles do form and begin to rise. These bubbles soon become so numerous that they cannot rise through water in the constricted tube, so they push the overlying water up and out of the geyser's neck. This first overflow of water typically precedes an eruption.

This overflow relieves the pressure far below the surface, allowing the super-heated water to flash into steam, expanding to about 1,700 times its liquid volume. This tremendous expansion shoots water up into the air—hence, the eruption. The eruption ends when the water reservoir is depleted, or the pressure is sufficiently relieved.

Yellowstone has two types of geysers—cone and fountain. The visible difference in the two is in the formation of geyserite (the grey, rock-like deposit that forms the cones and basins around geysers and hot springs). In a cone geyser, the geyserite has been deposited near the mouth of the geyser and builds up to form a cone. Thus, the mouth of the geyser is raised above ground level and the column of water rises in a steadily climbing and then falling sequence. White Dome is one such geyser. In a fountain geyser, the geyserite has formed a basin that holds the first overflow in a pool. The column of water rises out of it in consecutive bursts—like a fountain. Great Fountain, in the lower geyser basin, is one of these types of geysers. When it erupts, people take notice—and sometimes get wet. The scalding water cools rapidly so people aren't burned by these occasional showers. The massive bursts from Great Fountain Geyser reach 180 feet in the air.

TOP: *Great Fountain Geyser.* **BOTTOM LEFT:** *White Dome Geyser on Firehole Lake Drive.* **BOTTOM RIGHT:** *Geyserite deposits.*

TOP: *Aerial view of the Mink Creek Fire.* **MIDDLE:** *Helicopters, which could gather and dump large buckets of water, were a valuable part of the fire-fighting efforts.* **BOTTOM:** *Elk grazing in burned area near Madison.* **OPPOSITE:** *New growth is already apparent in a meadow near Madison in late October 1988.*

the fires of 1988

In 112 years of record keeping, 1988 was one of the driest years in Yellowstone's history. The drought, however, is only one of many circumstances that caused Yellowstone National Park to be the site of the largest natural fires in recorded history.

In 1972, park officials adopted a "natural-fire" policy in a portion of the park. By 1975 the policy extended to most of the park. This policy discourages human intervention in lightning-caused fires unless they pose a threat to human lives, property, or special features. The policy supports the contention that natural forest fires are essential for a healthy ecosystem.

Years without large fires led to an accumulation of dead material on the forest floors, and to acres of dry lodgepole pine trees. But it was drought, low humidity, and high winds that were the important factors in the 1988 fires.

In early summer, twenty of the lightning-caused fires were allowed to burn and 11 went out on their own. Park officials counted on the rains of June and July to suppress the rest, but, very little rain fell. Instead, unusually high winds and scores of additional lightning strikes compounded the blazes. Through the long, hot summer, thousands of specially drafted fire-fighters, with the aid of helicopters and airplanes, worked diligently to suppress flames that burned in many different spots. Over 100 million dollars were spent in the firefighting efforts, but the fires raged on their own terms until mid-September.

THE AFTERMATH

When the smoke finally cleared, rumors of Yellowstone's devastation turned out to be greatly exaggerated. Estimates suggest that the total burned area amounted to 1.38 million acres in and near Yellowstone. Of Yellowstone's 2.2 million acres, a maximum of 995,000 acres experienced some kind of burning. Remember, fires don't follow distinct boundaries, they burn along jagged lines in a patchwork fashion. Also, the *degree* of burning varies enormously, for example, trees aren't necessarily killed.

Yellowstone has survived many natural cataclysms over the years and the fires of 1988 were no exception. Consider Yellowstone's chief attractions—hydrothermal features that are unparalleled in the world, a profusion of varied wildlife, and the mystique of being the world's first national park. These features remain—unchanged by the fires. As does the awe-inspiring Grand Canyon of Yellowstone and magnificent Lake Yellowstone.

Naturalists believe that the fires will prove to have a reinvigorating effect on the forests and the species that inhabit them. In fact, grasses and shrubs will thrive in the forest floors, now full of nutrient-rich ash. By spring, brilliantly colored wildflowers will pop up and fast-growing aspen will take root; dead trees full of insects will provide food and nests for birds; and after decades, sunlight will finally reach the forest floors.

Park visitors will have the unique opportunity to observe firsthand how Mother Nature—not always beautiful or gentle—recovers from natural events. It is interesting to note that there is good evidence that widespread fires of this type occurred 200 to 400 years ago in Yellowstone.

Since its inception, Yellowstone National Park has been a trailblazer in the art and science of preserving nature, so it is no surprise that its "natural-fire" policy is undergoing solemn review following these fires. After many questions and issues are addressed, the likely result will be that if we choose to meddle with the ecological system, we must be prepared to deal with and accept the consequences.

The Grand Loop Road is a 142-mile highway in the middle of the park. It connects the access roads from the park's five entrances and encompasses Yellowstone's best-known recreational an scenic attractions. The 12-mile stretch between Norris and Canyon Village turns the road into a figure eight. The road within the park between the north entrance and Cooke City is open year-round, otherwise most park roads are closed from approximately November 1 to April 30 (depending upon snow conditions). Call park headquarters for information regarding snowcoach travel and regulations about snowmobiles.

In order to understand and appreciate what you're seeing along the Grand Loop Road, allow as much time as possible to stop at various roadside pull-outs and visitor centers and to take short walks from your car.

The following information highlights the main attractions and sites to be found on the Grand Loop Road, but it is by no means comprehensive. For further information, please refer to *Hamilton's Guide* (which includes a foldout map) for explanations of everything you'll be seeing along the way.

If you begin your journey on the Grand Loop Road at Mammoth Hot Springs (the park's northern entrance), your first stop should be the Horace M. Albright Visitor Center, which is housed in one of the magnificent stone buildings constructed during the time the U.S. Army protected and managed the park.

Before heading east from Mammoth on the Grand Loop Road, drive through town toward Mammoth Terraces. The first attraction is Liberty Cap, which is a naturally formed cone composed of calcium carbonate that is 37-feet high and 20 feet in diameter. The Mammoth Terraces are being formed as you watch—hot springs carry nearly 4,000 pounds of limestone deposits out of the earth each day.

The Upper Terraces area of Mammoth Hot Springs is accessible by car on a narrow one-way road that passes a series of impressive pools and scraggly, tenacious junipers. These gnarled trees may be the oldest living things in the park. This road rejoins the Grand Loop after a mile.

As you leave Mammoth on the Grand Loop Road, watch for wildlife and after crossing the bridge, look back for a different perspective of Mammoth Terraces. As striking in the distance as they are close up, imagine viewing this spectacle from horseback 100 years ago.

For a pleasant side trip and an opportunity to see wildflowers and perhaps deer and elk, watch for a spur road called Blacktail Plateau Drive, which leaves the Grand Loop Road 10 miles from Mammoth Hot Springs. Another side road, closer

CHAPTER•4

driving the grand loop

PREVIOUS PAGE, TOP: *Liberty Cap, an extinct geyser.* **BOTTOM:** *Sunset at Minerva Terrace at Mammoth Hot Springs.*

TOP: *Cow Elk with her calves.* **RIGHT:** *A wildflower-covered hillside on Blacktail Plateau.* **OPPOSITE:** *Grizzlies roam over large areas and have well-established trails.*

to Tower Junction, takes you to the Petrified Tree—a geological marvel. This redwood stump is enclosed by a fence and stands in the same spot where it grew 50 million years ago.

Sunrise or sunset in the Lamar Valley is the best time for viewing a variety of wildlife. Elk, deer, prong-horn antelope, bison, and coyote dot the Lamar expanse, and the sharp-eyed observer may even spot a grizzly. Binoculars and spotting scope are handy but not essential. Over the generations, Yellowstone animals have become less wary of automobiles, but remain suspicious of humans who don't keep their distance. Visitors are reminded that for their own safety and out of respect for wildlife they should keep a safe distance from park animals. People who do not follow this advice can be fined. Lamar Valley is also a superb spot for winter wildlife photog-raphy. The road to Tower Fall is carved out of the south face of a 500-foot gorge cut by the Yellowstone River. Use the turnouts and heed the barriers. Tower Fall, which drops 132 feet, and is distinguished by its sentinels of volcanic rock, was an important landmark for Indians in search of a crucial ford in the Yellowstone River.

The road up 8,859-foot Dunraven Pass has several stopping places, including a side road up the northwest flank of Mt. Washburn. The three-hour hike to the top of this 10,243-foot peak is well worth the effort and you may see bighorn sheep along the way. Either vista is a good place to see the effect of the 1988 fires. Blackened areas intermingle with untouched ones in patchwork fashion, revealing the arbitrary nature of forest fires. The view should temper any myth that the fires "destroyed" Yellowstone. Most is untouched.

Roads from Canyon Village lead to numerous vantage points overlooking the 1,500-foot-deep, 26-mile-long Grand Canyon of the Yellowstone. Grand View, Inspiration Point, and Artist Point, which inspired Thomas Moran's famous painting of the canyon, provide excellent scenic views of the canyon. There are short walks from the pull-outs and longer hikes along the canyon rim.

A walk down Uncle Tom's Trail to Lower Falls, a breathtaking perch directly in front of its 308-foot plunge, is an unforgettable experience.

Mineral oxides give the cliffs a multi-hued appearance that becomes brilliant in the ever-changing light. At certain angles, the sunlight creates rainbows in the mist.

Above the Upper Falls, the Yellowstone River is a placid, trout-filled river. (Only-catch-and-release fishing is allowed.) This area marks the beginning of Hayden Valley, formerly a lake bottom whose sediment has created a fertile landscape of subtle beauty. Its diverse habitats make it a natural wildlife sanctuary for coyotes, bison, and even grizzly bear. The valley is also home to a wide assortment of birds, including pelicans, hawks, a variety of ducks, and even an occasional great blue heron and bald eagle. This area is closed to fishing.

For your safety, stay on the roads and do not approach wildlife. Hayden Valley is a place to gaze at the horizon and to revel in the exquisiteness of the area.

Just below Hayden Valley is the Mud Volcano area, Yellowstone's most outrageous collection of thermal features. You can't miss it for the pervasive odor of rotten eggs, the steaming vents, and the hissing, sizzling pools. Be sure to take the boardwalk to observe Black Dragon's Caldron—you never know what will pop up next. This noisy, frothing pond first erupted during the winter of 1947-48.

In June or July, Le Hardy Rapids (three miles before Fishing Bridge) is a good spot to watch trout struggling

TOP: *An autumn morning on the Gibbon River.* **BOTTOM:** *Visitors can view the thermal areas from the many boardwalks that wind through them.* **OPPOSITE:** *Other park geysers may erupt higher, but none are as spectacular as Old Faithful.*

to jump above the rapids. Fishing is no longer allowed at Fishing Bridge because it is a prime spawning ground. Fishing Bridge is located near the outlet of Yellowstone Lake, the largest freshwater lake in the country at such a high elevation. It is roughly 20 miles long and 14 miles wide and has 110 miles of meandering shoreline and picnic spots galore. The museum at Fishing Bridge features exhibits on Yellowstone's wildlife and geology.

At West Thumb Geyser Basin, there is yet another collection of paint pots, fumaroles, and pools whose colors defy description. The blue of Abyss Pool is remarkable. There are also numerous hot springs and steam vents of all types and sizes.

Grant Village is off the Grand Loop Road, just two miles south of West Thumb. It offers a wide range of facilities and a visitor center/museum.

As you continue west on the Grand Loop Road, be sure to stop at Isa Lake. It is a small, gem-like lake on Craig Pass (8,262 feet) that straddles the Continental Divide, which means that its water flows to the Atlantic in one direction and to the Pacific in the other.

Once over Craig Pass, you'll go by an area that, on August 24, 1908, was the scene of "the greatest stagecoach robbery of the twentieth century." A bandit, who had waited patiently four and a half miles from the Upper Geyser Basin, held up 17 coaches and 174 passengers for a take of about $2,000. He was never caught, but some jewelry was found in the woods three years later.

Old Faithful, located in the Upper Geyser Basin, is the world's most famous geyser. True to its reputation, Old Faithful, on the average, spouts once every 60 to 80 minutes; rangers time each eruption with a stopwatch, as the duration of one eruption contains the secret to predicting the next.

With its majestic column of steam and spray, Old Faithful is a master performer whose moonlit burst can provide a romantic highlight to a Yellowstone trip; a noontime burst, photographed through a polarizing filter, will redefine your concept of "pure white."

Plan to spend as much time as possible exploring the Old Faithful area and Upper Geyser Basin. There are a few dozen thermal features within walking distance along the Firehole River. A network of boardwalks takes you through an amazing array of thermal features blowing surreal clouds of steam in the air. Ski and snowshoe treks and naturalist-led hikes around Geyser Hill Loop start from the Old Faithful Visitor Center.

Some of the most beautiful thermal areas in the park lie between Old Faithful and Firehole Lake Drive, a one-way side road that should not be missed. It makes a three-mile loop off the main road and passes White Dome, Pink Cone, Narcissus, and Steady geysers, and Firehole Lake, one of Yellowstone's largest hot pools. Great Fountain Geyser is here, and goes off every 6 to 10 hours. (The average is every 9½ hours.) Each eruption is a lengthy series of splashy, spasmodic fits accompanied by thousands of gallons of water surging over its colorful terraces.

Not far from the road, and half-hidden in steamy mists, are Fountain Paint Pots. These paint pots (also called mud volcanoes or mud springs) are the result of warm water decomposing surface rocks to form clay. Fumaroles, which are modified hot springs with such a limited water supply that the heat is constantly turning it to steam, can also be found in this area. Hissing and rumbling sounds are made as the steam rushes up the earth's mysterious underground plumbing system.

A boardwalk takes you by various geysers and springs and overlooks some of the park's most active geysers: Clepsydra, Spasm, and Jelly. Clepsydra Geyser has been spouting continuously except for a few short rests, ever since the 1959 earthquake.

Seven miles north of Fountain Paint Pots is an interesting two-mile side road that winds through a deep canyon with 800-foot-high black walls that have been formed by lava flows. This one-time Indian trail takes you by Firehole Cascades and Firehole Falls. Madison Junction marks the confluence of the Firehole and Gibbon rivers, creating the Madison River. The Grand Loop Road continues along the Gibbon River and past 84-foot-high Gibbon Falls. If one geyser basin is to be taken in on foot, Norris Geyser Basin may be the wisest choice. It's a wild-looking, primeval place, an intense concentration of fumaroles, geysers, mudpots, turbid pools, and eerie scenery. Its museum displays clear descriptions of how Yellowstone's plumbing works.

Norris is also the home of the Steamboat Geyser, which is currently the world's highest shooting geyser (380 feet). Steamboat Geyser performs minor eruptions regularly, but the big blows rarely happen; the most recent occurred, at this writing, in 1984. All the more reason to visit it with your camera—catch Steamboat Geyser erupting and you'll have captured the rarest shot in Yellowstone.

Roaring Mountain, a tilted font of hot springs and vents, was named at

the turn of the century for a particularly noisy steam vent. It fumes in silence these days, but nobody knows for sure how long it will remain silent. The abrupt black monolith two miles to the north is Obsidian Cliff. Native Americans flaked points and tools from the black, glassy volcanic rock.

Sheepeater Cliffs are named after a little-known tribe of Indians called the Sheepeaters. They were the only tribe to live in the Yellowstone area year-round. The cliffs of basalt columns are the result of a lava flow that cooled, forming geometric shapes.

If you have a sturdy vehicle, take the dirt road around Bunsen Peak for a superb, panoramic view of the mountains and plateaus in the northwest corner of Yellowstone and Osprey Falls on the Gardner River.

Coming full circle, the Grand Loop Road now drops back into Mammoth Hot Springs. You may wish to make a return visit on the one-way drive around the Upper Terraces to view the remarkable limestone formations before finishing your trip.

TOP: *Firehole Falls on the Firehole River.*
BOTTOM: *Travertine-covered terraces at Mammoth Hot Springs.*

what's doing indoors?

Inclement weather actually provides an opportunity to discover more about Yellowstone from the displays, programs, and books offered by the park's seven visitor centers and museums.

The Horace M. Albright Visitor Center at Mammoth, which was named for the influential superintendent who became director of the National Park Service, is located inside one of eight stone buildings that were built when this complex was known as Fort Yellowstone. These sturdy buildings were constructed in 1909 (The chapel was built in 1913.) as headquarters for the U.S. Army Cavalry, which managed and protected the park from 1886 to 1918.

Films and slide programs are shown free of charge in the center's auditorium. Artifacts dating to the park's first residents and explorers, both Indian and Caucasian, are on display, as are collections of works by painter Thomas Moran and photographer William Henry Jackson. Their work was instrumental in convincing Congress to create the world's first national park. A ranger is always on duty who is eager to answer questions and to point out places on the map you never knew existed.

The park is sprinkled with these smaller visitor centers, each with its own theme:

- Old Faithful's visitor center has displays that explain how geysers work. Rangers post eruption predictions constantly, and are assisted by visitors with fresh news about geyser activity.
- The visitor center at Canyon has displays that describe the area's natural history and geology.
- At Grant Village the visitor center features changing exhibits and a slide show about Yellowstone's heritage.
- Norris Museum offers graphic presentations that explain hydrothermal plumbing and describe the curious, colorful algae and bacteria that thrive in hot water.
- Madison Trailside Museum describes the history of Yellowstone and tells how it became a national park.
- Wildlife (especially birds) and geology are featured in the museum at Fishing Bridge.

Architecture of historic and aesthetic significance exists throughout the park. The dining room at Mammoth Hot Springs Hotel was renovated to resemble its original snazzy art-deco style, and the hotel's Map Room features a United States map where each state is represented by a different type of wood. This map, created when the hotel was built in the 1930s, portrays an era when railroads were the prominent means of cross-country travel.

Every Yellowstone concession offers two essentials for a rainy day—a store to browse for books and postcards, and a quiet corner to read and write. On the other hand, what better excuse to head for the Hamilton Store at Lake for a world-class milkshake?

ABOVE: *Horace M. Albright Visitor Center at Mammoth.*

ABOVE: *Mammoth Hot Springs Hotel is one of Yellowstone's prime spots for winter activities.*

yellowstone's "grand old ladies"

As befitting an environment where the concerns of humanity usually run a distant second to the demands of nature, most buildings in Yellowstone tend to blend into the landscape. At Norris Geyser Basin, consider the museum and the adjacent log structure. They are simple and sturdy, and were built in an unpretentious, rustic style that has been adopted by national parks everywhere.

Accustomed to such basic accommodations, Yellowstone visitors are often amazed when confronting Lake Hotel, Mammoth Hot Springs Hotel, and Old Faithful Inn. Year after year, Yellowstone's historic hotels extend hospitality that reflects a bygone era of gracious living to hundreds of thousands of people. So successful have they been that these "grand old ladies" are now considered important park landmarks in their own right—as much an integral part of Yellowstone as Old Faithful or the Minerva Terrace.

Yellowstone's earliest visitors had to be content with crude log structures and tent camps. The National Hotel, built in 1883 at Mammoth, was a definite improvement. The hotel was spacious for the time, but the management would frequently overbook so that as many as 500 guests would be left fighting for the 151 available rooms. Its ramshackle facade and red and green paint shocked the sensibilities of many park visitors.

It was Seattle architect Robert C. Reamer who later defined the high standards of architecture for which Yellowstone came to be known. The first big hotel was built in 1883 and was called the National. Reamer did plans for its renovation in 1911. In the 1930s the hotel was torn down and a new one—Mammoth Hot Springs Hotel—was built. This present-day hotel is an austere version of Greek Revival architecture—confident, understated, and roomy.

Lake Hotel and Old Faithful Inn are other examples of Reamer's work. The Lake Hotel, a stately structure on the shore of Yellowstone Lake, opened its doors in 1891. Its four-story, 300-foot facade features a neo-classical motif (added by Reamer), which is conspicuous yet unimposing. Fifty-foot Ionic columns support the porte cochere, where coaches once arrived to deposit tired, dusty, but grateful guests. It is worth a trip around Gull Point Drive to observe this majestic hotel from across Bridge Bay.

By 1904, Lake Hotel had grown from 80 to 210 rooms. However, the dawning of the automotive age meant that the hotel—a center of attraction for the Carriage Trade—began to fade in popularity. Its magnificent porte cochere entrance was abandoned for a more convenient rear door.

During the winter of 1980-81 a new concessioner, TW Recreational Services, Inc. and the National Park Service reversed the Lake Hotel's demise by updating fire and security systems. They subsequently began an ambitious restoration program.

It was during the winter of 1903-04 that Reamer constructed his masterpiece, Old Faithful Inn. Unlike the Lake, this hotel made a bold statement about its rustic surroundings through extensive use of native rock and timber. In fact, Old Faithful Inn is one of the largest log structures ever built.

Erecting this seven-story grand hotel over the course of a single Yellowstone winter, when temperatures seldom exceed 25 degrees and can drop to 30 below, was a major accomplishment in itself. Old Faithful Inn sits on a high spot of the Upper Geyser Basin a quarter mile from its namesake, the world's most famous geyser. The Inn's fireplace, 500 tons of lava rock piled 80 feet high, towers through a 64-foot-square lobby, itself a cavern of exposed beams and catwalks. The colossal wrought iron clock with its 14-foot pendulum and equally hefty fireplace tools (including a popcorn popper) were forged by a blacksmith on the spot.

Old Faithful Inn has been remodeled and expanded over the years. Originally 350 feet long, it is now over 800 feet long and has 350 rooms. As huge as it is, the hotel is dwarfed by the expanse of the surrounding geyser basin. Though it's hard to imagine Old Faithful Inn being built today, when park officials are more adamant than ever about man-made structures upstaging those of Mother Nature, it would be just as hard to imagine Yellowstone without Old Faithful Inn.

BACKGROUND PHOTO: *Old Faithful Inn, 1913.* **TOP:** *Guests enjoy sunshine and fresh air on the deck at Old Faithful Inn.* **BOTTOM:** *The stately Lake Hotel on the shore of Yellowstone Lake.*

Yellowstone National Park is a bounty of hidden lakes, volcanic ridges, over 1,000 miles of trails, and high plateaus drenched in colorful wildflowers. Those who take to the trails know that Yellowstone is far from crowded. Horse packers as well as backpackers could make a career out of exploring the park inside and out. Canoeists are welcome at Lewis, Shoshone, and Yellowstone lakes. Extreme caution should be used because the lake water is very cold and sudden changes in weather can occur.

Due to Yellowstone's volcanic nature, most trails involve little of the difficult climbing characteristic of the Rockies. This is still wild country, however, certainly no place to learn the art of backpacking. Before venturing into the backcountry, beware of these potential dangers: rapidly changing weather; swift streams; rockfalls; confrontations with wildlife, particularly protective mothers with their young; and *giardia lamblia,* a tenacious parasitic bacterium present in the water. Portable water filters are handy, but there is no better insurance than boiling drinking water for at least one minute. And in Yellowstone, particularly, hydrothermal features exist in many areas—not just along roadsides—and the adjacent turf cannot always support the weight of a person with a heavy pack.

Exploring bear country can be a remarkable experience, but one must be alert and cautious. Conflicts between bears and humans are rare and usually can be traced to ignoring the basic rules: do not make food accessible at night, and when you spot a bear give it all the room you can. And don't forget: hiking in bear country means taking a risk.

Rangers feel personally responsible for every person who enters the backcountry. Registration for overnight trips is mandatory, but permits are free. Campsites are limited. Reservations may be made up to 48 hours in advance and must be made in person at a ranger station. The permit process allows rangers to know where people are in the backcountry, but most importantly, to give them valuable safety information. They seldom stop anyone, but are available to give advice that could ensure a safe adventure.

Rangers have up-to-date information about trail conditions and wildlife concerns. Some areas of the park are closed when a particular food source (spawning trout, elk calves, or carrion) has drawn bears into that area. In the winter, the Central Plateau is off limits so as not to disturb its concentration of wildlife. Boating is allowed in few places, again in deference to wildlife.

CHAPTER • 5

exploring the backcountry

PREVIOUS PAGE, TOP: *Giant red paintbrush.* **BOTTOM:** *Thunderstorm over "The Trident," a series of rock formations more than 10,000 feet high.*

TOP: *Norris Geyser Basin.*
BOTTOM: *Guided pack trips are a fun way to explore Yellowstone's backcountry.*
OPPOSITE: *Autumn aspens in Lamar Valley.*

Springtime in the backcountry is marked by high waters and a blanket of muddy snow. Cow moose can be seen teaching their knock-kneed calves about the world. Until June, few trails of any length are free of fords and deep drifts so day trips at lower elevations are more enjoyable. Try the Fairy Falls Trail at Lower Geyser Basin (Some areas are frequently closed at this time of year due to bison calving and grizzly activity.), the trail to Lone Star Geyser near Old Faithful, or the Yellowstone River Trail.

Summertime, beginning in late June and lasting through August, brings dry trails, endless varieties of wildflowers, and 70-degree days and 35-degree nights. This is Yellowstone's prime season. Carpets of pink, blue, and white phlox and scarlet Indian paintbrush blossom, and you may catch the scent of mint as you walk through the undergrowth. Notably, there is neither poison ivy nor poison oak.

The fall season begins in September and lasts until much of the park closes around the end of October. The most stable, or at least the most predictable weather, comes in the fall. A tinge of winter makes stands of aspen turn from green to shimmery gold to bare in a week's time. Clusters of rye grass emanate yellow, a color that seems to change the sky itself. Fall mornings in Yellowstone bring backlit frosts, bracing air, and bugling elk.

Trailheads are everywhere, and keep in mind that one need not start in the middle of the park. Several trails begin in the bordering national forests—Bridger-Teton, Shoshone, Targhee, and Gallatin—but permits are still required. Some possibilities include:

- Altitude seekers might head for the Gallatin Range, in the northwest corner of the park. At 55 million years old, these are the Yellowstone Plateau's oldest mountains. The trail to the top of 10,336-foot Mt. Holmes ends at a fire lookout. A 25-mile trip up Indian Creek over Big Horn Pass (9,100 feet) and down to the Gallatin River, and the park's east boundary leads to some fine fishing.
- From Tower, a 16-mile trip up Specimen Ridge culminates at 9,614-foot Amethyst Mountain before dropping down into the wildlife-rich Lamar Valley.
- The Pitchstone Plateau in the southwest corner of the park was virtually unexplored until the 1920s. Even today, it sees little traffic although it is the site of the park's most recent volcanic activity (75,000 years ago). A 32-mile trail from Lone Star Geyser to Bechler River Ranger Station includes many waterfalls and some hot springs. A pleasant side trip can be made to a geyser basin on Shoshone Lake.
- The Absaroka (pronounced ab-SOR-ka) Range forms Yellowstone's eastern border and includes most of its loftiest peaks. Near the highest point, the 11,358-foot Eagle Peak, Yellowstone's border meets those of the Washakie and Teton wilderness areas.

Whether reached from the South Entrance road 35 miles away or through Cody, Wyoming and the Shoshone National Forest on the other side, this is as far back as backcountry gets in the lower 48 states. The Trident, a series of abrupt rock formations towering over 10,000 feet, have been observed by very few.

Winter campers enjoy Yellowstone's hydrothermal features with added pleasure albeit added risk. Trails that are well marked during the summer are all but obliterated during the winter. Beware that if you follow tracks, they can be covered by fresh snow at any time.

It may be tempting to think of hydrothermal areas as a way to combat sub-zero air temperatures, but in fact, they are too hot (and illegal) for bathing, and the steam generated makes a person wet and vulnerable to chilling. It is permissible to bathe in cold streams that receive hot water runoff.

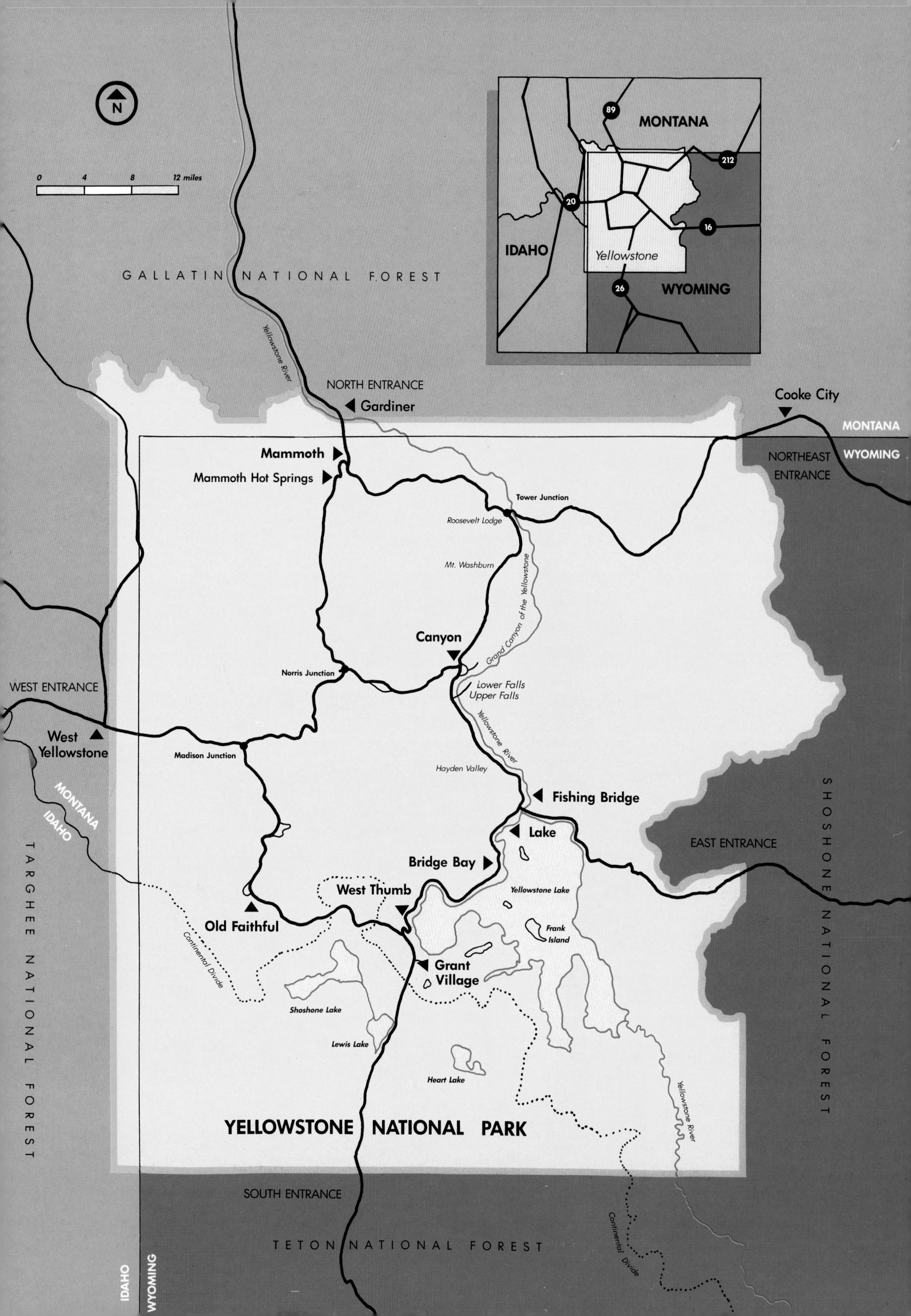
N
0
4
8
12 miles
GALLATIN NATIONAL FOREST
Yellowstone River
MONTANA
IDAHO
WYOMING
Yellowstone
89
212
20
16
26
NORTH ENTRANCE
Gardiner
Cooke City
MONTANA
WYOMING
NORTHEAST ENTRANCE
Mammoth
Mammoth Hot Springs
Tower Junction
Roosevelt Lodge
Mt. Washburn
Grand Canyon of the Yellowstone
Canyon
Norris Junction
Lower Falls
Upper Falls
WEST ENTRANCE
West Yellowstone
Madison Junction
Yellowstone River
Hayden Valley
MONTANA
IDAHO
Fishing Bridge
Lake
EAST ENTRANCE
Bridge Bay
West Thumb
Yellowstone Lake
Old Faithful
Frank Island
Continental Divide
Grant Village
Shoshone Lake
Lewis Lake
Heart Lake
Yellowstone River
TARGHEE NATIONAL FOREST
SHOSHONE NATIONAL FOREST
YELLOWSTONE NATIONAL PARK
SOUTH ENTRANCE
TETON NATIONAL FOREST
Continental Divide
IDAHO
WYOMING